Social Media for Musicians

Connecting on a Global Scale

Table of Contents

Music can change the world because it can change people.

— Bono

Chapter 1. Introduction

Dive into the melodic realm of social media with our Special Report, "Social Media for Musicians: Connecting on a Global Scale." Walk with us across digital platforms and shake hands with potential worldwide audiences, all craving for your unique harmonies. This is no dry, technical dossier; instead, it's a vibrant symphony of useful tips, inspiring success stories, and innovative strategies designed for artists like you! Get ready to amplify your digital presence, transform casual listeners into loyal fans, and stage performances in the virtual world that resonate globally. Tune up, purchase this report today, and begin your joyful journey of transcending global boundaries through the power chords of social media!

Chapter 2. Setting the Stage: An Introduction to Social Media for Musicians

Let the curtain rise and the lights dim as we embark on our melodious voyage through the fascinating world of social media, specifically tailored for musicians. This thrilling journey is sure to be a captivating exploration, a blend of technology and artistry that can revolutionize the way musicians connect, share, and thrive in the digital age.

2.1. Understanding the Dynamics of Social Media

The advent of social media has undoubtedly created revolutionary changes in the way we communicate, engage, and even do business. Far from being simply platforms for connecting with friends and family, social media networks have emerged as powerful tools for building a global presence. As a musician, understanding the dynamics of this digital universe is crucial.

Leveraging social media allows you to convert simple interactions into meaningful connections. Imagine a digital venue where you're not limited by geography or time-zones. Your audience could be sipping coffee in Toronto, having dinner in Beijing, or dancing the night away in Rio de Janeiro, and yet, with just a click, they can engage with your music, becoming an active part of your artistic journey.

2.2. The Fusion of Music and Social Media

Music and social media form a harmonious partnership, establishing an insightful and interactive symphony that the digital world dances to. As a musician, social media offers you a global platform where you can showcase your talent to a diverse and vast audience eagerly waiting to discover fresh beats.

Think of social media as a grand stage where you can connect with your fans on a personal level – a virtual stage that extends to the ends of the Earth. Your music can now reach audiences that were previously unreachable, your rhythms reverberating through every corner of the globe.

Every social media platform, be it Facebook, Instagram, YouTube, or Twitter, is a thriving digital hub filled with potential fans. By sharing your musical voyage on these platforms, you can gain exposure, engage listeners, and cultivate a loyal fan base that spans continents.

2.3. The Power of Digital Storytelling

One of the most fascinating aspects of social media is its ability to weave powerful narratives around your music. Your audience is no longer just interested in the final product; they yearn for the story behind every melody, every performance, every collaboration.

Social media empowers you to share these stories, taking your audience on a captivating journey from the seed of an idea to the blossoming of a rhythm. Sharing behind-the-scenes footage, discussing inspirations or challenges, and interacting with fans are all ways to engage your audience and make them feel a part of your musical vision.

2.4. Navigating the Social Media Landscape

For those who are new to the world of social media or have yet to fully explore its potential, the vast array of options and tactics can seem daunting. Not every platform may be right for you, and rightly identifying which ones are conducive to your growth can be a task in itself.

But fear not! This guide will help you navigate this vibrant jungle, pointing out the 'must-haves', 'nice-to-haves', and 'definitely avoid' aspects of the social media landscape. It will also delve into specifics, providing tips on how to utilize each platform's unique features and quirks to your advantage.

Welcome, dear musician, to the mesmerizing world of social media. This isn't just about learning to use a tool; this is about harnessing the power of connectivity, amplifying your music, and resonating with crowds around the globe. So, pick up your instrument, clear your throat, and get ready to perform on the grandest stage of all - the World Wide Web!

Chapter 3. Crafting Your Digital Persona: Developing an Engaging Online Presence

In an era defined by digital connection and interactivity, as a musician you find yourself presented with not only the challenge of perfecting your art but also the task of crafting an engaging online persona. This persona will become the digital face of your music, a visual and textual representation of your brand that interacts with audiences across the globe. It's the art of blending individuality, charm, authenticity, and industry insight into a tantalizing symphony that resonates with your digital audiences. So, where do you begin this arduous yet rewarding journey? Let's dive in.

3.1. Understanding Your Artistic Identity

Before you can paint your digital self, you must first understand your artistic identity. This is the core of who you are as an artist, your music style, your values, your story, and your aspirations. Grasp the essence of your music and translate it into a narrative. Are you a pop prodigy intent on shaking up the industry? Are you championing a forgotten music genre? Silhouetting your artistic identity reveals the colors you'll use to paint your digital persona.

3.2. Setting the Tone: Authenticity & Consistency

The core principles guiding your online presence should undeniably be authenticity and consistency. Authenticity ensures that you stay true to your artistic essence while consistency creates familiarity with your fans. Always be genuine in your interactions, exhibit your unique personality, and showcase the raw emotion that drives your music. Meanwhile, ensure consistency in post schedules, engagement, visual aesthetics, language, tone, amongst others.

3.3. Channeling Your Inner Storyteller

Engaging online presence involves weaving compelling narratives. Be it your journey into the music world, the inspiration behind songs, or the antics occurring in tour life, people enjoy a good story. Use relatable narratives to engage with your audience, making them feel a part of your journey. Sprinkling these stories across your digital interaction reinforces brand identity and deepens emotional connection with fans.

3.4. Crafting Your Visual Identity

Your visual identity is a crucial aspect of your online persona. From color schemes to typographies, from album covers to your Instagram feed — every visual element should radiate an aspect of your music. Consistency in these elements creates a visual language that fosters brand recognition.

3.5. Strategic Content Curation

Develop a strategic content plan with the intent of maintaining a balanced mix of promotional and casual engagement content. While it is necessary to promote your new releases or concerts, becoming overly promotional can tarnish your connection with fans. Balance it out with backstage snapshots, fan interactions, glimpses of your personal life or even your thoughts on relevant societal issues.

3.6. Engagement: The Key to Sustainability

Merely posting great content does not cut it; you must engage with your followers. Respond to their comments, host regular Q&A sessions, go live before a big event, or even dedicate songs to them. Building an engaged and committed online community boosts your music's reach and immersion.

3.7. Navigation through Challenges

The dreamy digital landscape is not without its thorns. Negative comments, internet trolls, and stringent platform policies may dampen your digital experience. It is crucial to develop a thick skin, remain respectful and steer clear from heated controversies. Always consult platform-specific guidelines before posting to avoid unnecessary complications.

3.8. Celebrating Milestones

Celebrate and share both personal and professional milestones with your digital family. Did you just finish recording your latest album? Have you hit a significant follower count? Sharing these moments imbues a sense of community and makes fans feel like they are part of your journey.

In the end, crafting an engaging digital persona is an art as profound as the music you create. It doesn't happen overnight but requires patience, persistence, creativity, authenticity, and a deep understanding of your artistic self and your audience's needs. So, set out today, start painting this digital portrait, and let your music reverberate across the digital realm.

Chapter 4. Sound Waves in Digital Sea: Choosing the Right Social Media Platforms

As an aspiring artist, the importance of choosing adequate platforms to showcase your talent can't be overstated. Your choice of a channel paints a mental image of your art in the viewers' minds and determines how your music will be discovered, shared, and appreciated. In this vast digital ocean teeming with infinite possibilities, making the right choice isn't always straightforward. This chapter is designed to serve as a compass to guide you through the cacophony of limitless digital channels.

4.1. Assess Your Target Audience

The first step in navigating through the digital sea involves understanding who you're trying to reach. How old are they? What's their preferred platform for discovering new music? What time are they most active? The importance of directing your sound waves towards the right demographic can't be overstated. Using social media metrics and analytics tools might prove crucial in decoding your target audience's preferences.

Implement survey tools on your pre-existing platforms to understand the online behavior of your audience. Millennials may utilize Instagram and Spotify heavily, while older generations might prefer Facebook and YouTube. Tailoring your presence according to your audience preference, therefore, remains paramount in carving an impactful digital presence.

4.2. Selecting The Right Platform

Once you've understood your audience, it narrows down the sea of available platforms, making selection less overwhelming. Here's a breakdown of popular platforms and their respective benefits:

- **Facebook**: Helps in establishing a diverse digital presence due to its widespread audience. It allows for longer posts, sharing concert dates, posting updates, and linking to music videos or song downloads. Facebook Live feature enables live interactions with your fans.

- **Instagram**: Ideal for younger audiences. Allows artists to give snapshots of their lives and journey, creating a personal connection with fans. IGTV feature for longer videos provides an excellent platform for showcasing live performances, behind-the-scenes footage, etc.

- **Twitter**: Best for brief updates and quick interactions with fans. Great for trending topics or joining relevant conversations through hashtags.

- **YouTube**: Prime platform for sharing high-quality videos. Also acts as a music discovery platform, with an enormous and varied user base.

- **TikTok**: A platform where creativity thrives, especially fame with younger demographics. Gives an opportunity to ride trends, create challenges, or share bite-sized performances.

Remember, not all platforms have to be utilized. Focusing on a few platforms catering to your audience will generate higher engagement.

4.3. Developing a Consistent Brand Image

Regardless of the platform(s) you choose, consistency in messages, themes, and aesthetics is key. Your audience will expect consistent quality and style wherever they interact with your brand online. Therefore, synchronizing your feeling, tone, and visuals across different platforms sets a standard for your brand and makes you easily identifiable. Consolidating visuals, messages, along with your music, creates a holistic brand experience for your audience.

4.4. Understanding Platform-Specific Etiquette

Each social media platform has its unwritten rules and etiquette. Twitter values brevity and quick wit, while Instagram appreciates quality visuals and clever use of hashtags. Understanding and adapting these can differentiate successful social media usage from a failed effort.

4.5. Continual Exploration and Adaptation

Processes should be iterative. New platforms emerge, and old ones evolve. Following trends and constantly re-assessing your strategy keeps you ahead in the ever-evolving digital landscape.

In conclusion, choosing the right platforms is not a process to rush. It necessitates careful thought, meticulous research, and continuous reassessment. Be patient, modify as needed, and continue refining your choices to align with the ebb and flow of the digital ocean. Select your platforms wisely and let your music traverse the world, reaching out to those waiting to dive deep into the mesmerizing symphony that is uniquely yours.

Chapter 5. Capturing the Perfect Pitch: Content Creation and Posting Strategies

In this fascinating exploration of musical content creation, we begin our journey by understanding that as an artist, you are not just merely involved in the production of sounds, but the creation of an experience, an immersive engagement for your audience. To successfully translate this to the digital landscape, artists must navigate a voyage of discovering their unique path in content development and maintain consistently effective posting practices.

5.1. Developing Your Content Strategy: The Core of Your Online Persona

At the heart of successful social media for musicians is a sound content strategy. This strategy should be a beacon, carefully guiding and informing all your creative decisions. It resonates with the sentiments of your music, mirrors your personality, and embodies your vision. Remember, the lifeblood of your online presence relies heavily on showcasing your authentic self. Meanwhile, you must also blend it with what your audience desires.

To synthesize a melody that strikes a chord with both artists and fans requires a deep understanding of your audience's demographics, consumption habits, preferences, and more. Engaging in social listening, seeking insights from analytical tools, and proactively observing discussions can provide you with a wealth of information to extract and craft a well-tuned content strategy.

5.2. The Art of Content Creation: Types, Formats, and Consistency

As an artist, your most potent tool at your disposal is your creativity. When it comes to content creation, ensure that you vary your types and formats of content to keep your listeners engaged and captivated. Here, we explore several options:

1. Performance videos - Raw, organic footages of you creating music, live shows, rehearsals, or jam sessions. Such content provides an intimate look into your world of music creation.

2. Behind-the-scenes content - This showcases your creative process, your inspirations, your challenges, your triumphs. Sharing these moments humanizes you and foster strong connections with your audience.

3. Blogs or Vlogs - Share your experiences, thoughts, and journey. Consider creating collaborations with other musicians for joint content or interview-format pieces.

4. Educational content - Leveraging your skill can be done by posting tutorials or guides related to music, instruments, or techniques.

5. User-generated content - Encourage your fans to post their experiences with your music, covers, or remixes.

When it comes to consistency, understand it's not just about frequency but also about maintaining a constant voice, theme, and quality. Consistency helps to create familiarity, and with familiarity comes trust and loyalty from your audience.

5.3. Mastering the Posting Cadence: The What, When, and How Frequently?

The frequency, timing, and kind of posts you make play a crucial role in your success on social media. There's no one-size-fits-all solution, but there are general guidelines that can be customized to fit your specific needs.

1. Post consistently - Consistency helps improve visibility, fosters familiarity, and builds audience anticipation.

2. Experiment with timings - Usage patterns can vary among different social platforms and audience. Use analytical tools to understand when your audience is most active.

3. Mix it up: Balance - As important as it is to promote your music, it's just as essential to have a varied mix that ranges from promotional, informative to interactive content.

Remember, quality always trumps quantity. It's always better to have one high-quality post that resonates with your audience than multiple posts that are off-key.

5.4. Tuning Your Caption: Making Every Word Count

Never underestimate the power of a well-crafted caption. Your captions should draw the audience in, making them an integral part of your narrative. Use persuasive language, inject humor, ask questions, or share personal anecdotes to keep your posts engaging.

Creating content for social media may feel like walking on a tight-wipe at times, but with the right strategy, creating the perfect pitch becomes second nature. The balance between authenticity and audience appeal, creativity, and consistency, as well as presence and promotion, will harmonize your journey in the exciting world of social media for musicians.

Chapter 6. Harmonizing the Crowd: Engagement and Community Building

The art of engaging with your community and building a tribe of loyal fans is no small feat within the digital landscape of social media. It takes a symphony of carefully orchestrated strategies and fine-tuned interactions to keep your audience engaged and make them feel like an essential part of your musical journey.

6.1. Understanding Your Fans

To harmonize the crowd, the first step is to understand who your fans are and what resonates with them. You need to identify the demographic profile of your followers—their age group, their geographical location, their tastes in music, and more. To obtain this valuable information, social media sites like Instagram and Twitter offer audience insights tools that make it easy to learn about your fan base.

Take the time to analyze these insights, look for trends, and check what content has the highest engagement. Your aim should be to engage your listeners by connecting with them on a personal level, asking them questions, conducting polls, or creating content that aligns with their interests. Such methods not only boost engagement but also foster a sense of community around your music.

6.2. Choosing the Right Tone

Communication is a crucial aspect of community building, and the tone you use will significantly affect how your music is perceived by your audience. Are you formal, relaxed, humorous, or serious? Your tone should mirror both your music and your personality. Authenticity is the cornerstone of success; fans appreciate artists who are genuine and true to their ethos.

Though it's essential to maintain professionalism, don't be afraid to show the person behind the music. Sharing stories from your life and your musical journey can strengthen the bond with your community. It provides them a window to your world, relatable touchpoints, and demonstrates your shared love for music.

6.3. Hosting Live Q&A

Live sessions are an excellent tool to interact with your audience in real-time, answer their queries and provide a sneak-peek into your life as a musician. It encourages fans to participate actively, bridging the gap between you and your followers. Utilize features like Instagram Live or Facebook Live to host these sessions, discussing everything from your creative process to upcoming performances.

6.4. Building a Team

A successful social media presence is often attributed to not just one individual, but a team working behind the scenes. If your budget allows, consider hiring a social media manager or a digital marketing team to help you strategize content, manage engagement, and grow your following. Having a dedicated team will ensure consistency in your social media postings and interactions.

6.5. Organizing Contests and Giveaways

One fun and effective way to boost engagement is by running social media contests or giveaways. It can boost new follows, shares, likes, comments, and overall visibility. You can give away signed albums, concert tickets, merchandise or even exclusive experiences like a virtual meet and greet. While doing this, ensure you comply with the terms and conditions of the respective social media platform.

6.6. Collaborating with Other Artists

Collaborations are a valuable way to reach out to a broader audience and forge connections within the music community. Partner with artists who complement your music, and promote each other's work on your platforms. Cross-promotion not only provides fresh content to your followers but also introduces you to new potential fans.

6.7. Consistency is Key

Last but not least, consistency is essential for building a robust social media presence and engaging community. Regularly posting and interacting with your fans will keep your music at the forefront of their minds. Match the frequency of your posts with your audience's preferences and your ability to create high-quality content. Remember, quality should never be sacrificed for quantity.

This extensive dive into engagement and community building forms the crux of leveraging social media effectively as a musician. It demands time, patience, and sincerity, but the symphony that unfolds will be worth the effort, enabling you to touch the hearts of your audience, not just through your music, but also through meaningful and treasured interactions.

Chapter 7. Solo to Symphonies: Collaborations and Networking on Social Media

As the grand lyricist of your digital narrative, one crucial aspect of navigating the social media realm extends beyond merely creating unique tunes and broadcasting them to a global audience. The ingenious tool of collaboration with fellow musicians and the strategic application of networking form a vital coda in your symphony of social media success. Comprehending this marvel is like mastering the chords of a complex melody; it can transform a solo performance into a global orchestra.

7.1. The Chorus of Collaboration

Collaboration is a powerful mechanism that musicians can harness to increase their influence and expand their reach on social media platforms. The essence of collaboration transcends the simple connotation of working together to produce or create music. It propagates the sharing of ideas, resources, audiences, and most importantly, the sonorous harmonization of talents that elevate a piece of music from ordinary to extraordinary.

Consider collaborations as duels where instead of competing against each other, musicians team up to sweep the audience off their feet. Not only do they become a domain to flex creative muscles, but they also manifest as a golden opportunity to gain new fans from the collaborator's fan base, and vice versa. Imagine collaborating with a musician having a significant following. The possibility of being discovered by this whole new demographic can radically elevate your online presence and fan-base.

7.2. Networking: A Rhythm that Resonates

Though akin to collaboration, networking brings with it another set of advantages. Networking, in a nutshell, is the exchange of information and ideas amongst individuals with similar interests. At its core, networking is about building authentic and mutually beneficial relationships over periods.

For a musician in the virtual world, networking can occur with peers, influencers, industry leaders, producers, or event organizers. A broad and well-connected network can provide access to higher-profile event participation, key industry insights, and shout-outs from influential figures within the music scene - all of which help enhance your social credibility and digital reach. The networking ripples then bounce back to your music, creating resounding waves that attract more listeners.

7.3. Strategies for Effective Collaborations and Networking

In the realm of social media, the effectiveness of collaborations and networking hinges significantly on the strategies employed. Here are some noteworthy strategies that can be beneficial for musicians piecing together their digital strategy:

1. **Identify Potential Collaborators:** The first step is identifying musicians who complement your style and audience. You're not merely looking for someone with a large number of followers. Instead, seek artists who share a similar genre, followership, or music ethos with you. The collaboration should feel organic to both sets of fans, keeping them engaged and curious.

2. **Reach Out and Express Interest:** The next step is to initiate a

connection. This could be done via social media messages, emails, or mutual contacts. Clearly express why you want to collaborate and articulate the mutual benefits that both parties would accrue from such collaboration.

3. **Mutual Promotion:** Utilize your social media platforms to cross-promote your combined work. It can be through casual shout-outs on Instagram stories, Twitter Retweets, Facebook Shares, or even YouTube collaborations. Make sure that both parties are equally dedicated to the promotional efforts.

4. **Participation in Online Communities:** Online music communities thrum with a wealth of networking opportunities. Engage in discussion forums, participate actively in star-hosted live events or webinars, and don't shy away from expressing your views on relevant issues. Such activities may draw the attention of potential collaborators and industry influencers.

5. **Formal Networking Opportunities:** Don't underestimate the power of formal networking opportunities such as online music conferences, webinars, and industry events. Such platforms may provide you with warm introductions to high profile contacts and potential influencers who can be pivotal in your career trajectory.

6. **Establish a Genuine Connection:** Networking isn't merely about taking; it's about establishing an authentic connection. Share their work, appreciate their efforts, and extend support during challenging times. By fostering a feeling of genuine connection, people will be more inclined to reciprocate, thereby creating a more potent networking impact.

Remember, collaborations and networking are not the magic potions that instantly propel you to instant stardom. Like every good composition, they need time, patience, consistency, and endless attempts at striking the perfect chord. However, the rewards are indeed worthwhile. So dive into this mesmeric realm of networked music and allow the symphony of collaboration to play the perfect melody to your digital success.

Chapter 8. Viral Beats: Leveraging Trends for Increased Impact

The magical world of social media moves at a breakneck speed, spiraling upwards on the wings of trends. These trends wield an extraordinary influence. Like a viral earworm, a trend can spread across the globe, elevating your music and your brand to unprecedented heights. Leverage this carefully for increased impact in the auditory battlefield of the digital age, and you may well find yourself the conductor of an energetic symphony of clicks, likes, shares, and applause.

8.1. The Virality Phenomenon

Virality is a vast and somewhat mercurial notion, operating at the intersection of culture, timing, appeal and often more unsuspecting factors. It's a fascinating phenomenon, but also one that can seem elusive and difficult to harness deliberately. The base content can be a video, picture, text, or of course, a powerful melody. When this content captures the collective digital imagination, it explodes onto the global stage, piggybacking on the power of shares, retweets, remixes and references. Leveraging this force requires a deep understanding of trends and the ability to pivot, iterate and create fast enough to ride the wave when it starts to swell.

8.2. Recognizing Trending Waves in the Sea of Social Media

Keeping your finger on the pulse of social trends often means a diet of constant social media consumption, punctuated by careful observation and analysis. It involves processes as nuanced as listening to the changing musical tastes and predilections of the audience, to as broad as tuning into global cultural shifts as they echo across digital landscapes.

Understanding the cultural humor of memes, the viral dance routines on TikTok, or the thematic undercurrents within Twitter's frenzied discussions can hint at opportunities to create music that resonates with these movements. Remember, in the age of digital immediacy, humor, novelty and relatability prove powerful factors in initiating a viral chain of shares.

8.3. Syncing Your Rhythms with Viral Beats

Aligning your musical creations with trending themes can dramatically massage the virality potential of your content. For instance, incorporating the latest trending dance moves in your music video, or structuring a new song around a viral catchphrase can amplify your reach. Sometimes, the simpler the better – the magic lies in embedding your music seamlessly within a trending conversation, finding a balance where your music both contributes to and benefits from the momentum of the trend.

Plenty of musicians have crafted engaging 'theme songs' for trending social media challenges, significantly enhancing their visibility. It's like leading a mass digital choir where every participant sings, dances, or nods along with your tune, playing their part in carrying your melody to every corner of the digital world.

8.4. Amplifying Your Beats: The Role of Influencers, Editors and Curated Playlists

In the social media realm, amplification comes through sharing, and a share from an account with a significant following can initiate the domino effect leading to virality. Collaborating with established social media figures, reaching out to influencers in your genre, or even having your music featured in curated playlists or by 'mood editors' can lead to sudden, phenomenal upticks in your music's reach.

For instance, getting your music used in a popular Youtuber's video or a popular influencer's Instagram story can springboard your beats straight into new listener groups. Much like a conductor leading the orchestra, a shout-out from an influencer can profoundly impact the direction and pace of your music's online journey.

8.5. Leveraging Viral Trends: Case Studies

Chapters are punctuated with case studies to create a vivid sense of the power and potential of leveraging trends creatively. Emulating successful strategies or using them as innovative launching pads can guide emerging musicians to join this digital melody. The case studies detail how musicians ingeniously seized trending waves, turned them to their advantage and in so doing skillfully boosted their social media prominence.

8.6. Viral Beats and Longevity: Moving Beyond the 15 Minutes of Fame

The nature of viral trends is transient. It combusts brilliantly, but the glow often fades just as quickly. Thus, how you leverage these trends for lasting impact is crucial. It requires a thoughtful balance between participating in trends and maintaining the individuality and consistency of your musical style.

One successful strategy is to think of viral successes as a stepping stones, rather than the destination. Let them be unique introductions, attracting a wider audience to not just the viral content, but to your overall body of work. Use these opportunities to draw listeners to your music, inviting them to explore and appreciate your extant and future compositions.

In conclusion, when trends are laced with your unique musical notes, they become more than ephemeral viral occurrences. They can morph into powerful introductions, pitching your harmonies to the world and turning momentary listeners into a loyal, engaged fanbase. Even in a theater whose stage is constantly morphing and whose spotlight flits ceaselessly- the internet - your music, your beats can narrate compelling stories that the digital world will stop to listen to. The orchestra is all set and the audience is waiting; it's time to make the world sway to your digital symphony.

Chapter 9. Lessons from the Spotlight: Case Studies of Successful Music Social Media Campaigns

We kick-start our guiding expedition with an exploration into the world of successful social media campaigns run by musicians, bands, and their creative teams. Having traversed the avenues of planning your social media image, selecting the right platforms, and fostering audience relationships, the next natural course of direction would be to look at those who have mastered these aspects and reaped the rewards. In this chapter, we spotlight some musical ensembles that have hit the right social media pitch, causing the chords of success to reverberate across the digital world.

9.1. The "Beyoncé" Surprise Album Launch

In November 2013, multi-platinum, Grammy-winning artist Beyoncé released her self-titled visual album "Beyoncé" without prior notice or promotion. A rock has landed in the digital sea, and its ripple effects are still being studied for their unique, disruptive impact. Beyoncé's surprise album drop was more than a marketing ploy. It was a maverick move noteworthy for how it harnessed social media to rewrite the rules of music distribution and promotion.

The album was released exclusively on iTunes; the artist used her Instagram account - boasting millions of followers - to announce its availability. That single Instagram post was an ignition spark that set off a wildfire of shares, likes, and comments; it also translated to strong album sales. Within three days, "Beyoncé" sold nearly 830,000 copies worldwide—an impressive feat in the digital age.

From this case, musicians can learn the power of leveraging an existing substantial follower base and the element of surprise. While it's true that not every artist possesses the star power of Beyoncé, they can still create engaging, unexpected content that generates similar excitement and interest among their audience.

9.2. Old Town Road: Leveraging the TikTok Wave

Lil Nas X's 'Old Town Road' is an unmissable example of social media's potential role in viral music promotion. The catchy song entered the collective cultural consciousness not through the traditional channels of music distribution, but through the Short Video App - TikTok. Users started creating videos with the 'Yeehaw Challenge,' driving immense popularity and paving the track's way to a whopping nineteen weeks at number one on the Billboard Hot 100.

This multifaceted campaign demonstrates the efficiency of integrating a social media platform, particularly one aimed at a younger demographic, as a critical pillar in your music promotion strategy. Embarking on a similar journey, musicians can discover unconventional ways to engage audiences and, more significantly, become trendsetters themselves.

9.3. BTS ARMY: Nurturing a Loyal Fanbase

South Korean boy band BTS (Bangtan Sonyeondan), often called the "Beatles of the 21st Century," built their colossal fanbase mainly through social media. Their dedicated social media strategy included regular vlogs (video blogs) about their life behind the scenes, interactive engagements with fans, and teasers of their works in progress shared on platforms like Twitter, YouTube, and Vlive.

Their strategy has created the loyal BTS ARMY (Adorable Representative M.C. for Youth), a fanbase that spans continents and defies cultural barriers. Their social media strategy is a model for using authenticity and consistent interaction to cultivate a passionate, loyal fan following.

9.4. Coldplay's Virtual Concerts: Concerts in Quarantine

As the world went under pandemic-imposed lockdowns, musicians grappled with the challenge of staying connected with their audiences. Here, Coldplay stood out with their #TogetherAtHome concert series. Band frontman Chris Martin performed live from his home, broadcasting it on Instagram live and later uploading the performances on YouTube.

The #TogetherAtHome series was a perfect blend of audience engagement and adaptiveness to the new normal. Musicians can learn the importance of showing resilience and leveraging technology to reach an audience even when traditional concert venues are not an option.

These case studies provide a varied repertoire for musicians looking to harness the power of social media. Each story resonates with a salient theme, whether it's leveraging trends as Lil Nas X did, fostering a loyal audience like BTS, masterfully using the surprise factor like Beyoncé, or adapting to a changing world like Coldplay did. The common underlying note among these diverse tunes is the effective use of social media as a force majeur in the music industry.

Evidence of its impact can be found throughout the music world, from surprise album drops to viral TikTok trends, from crossing cultural boundaries to creating virtual concerts. Through it all, social media is helping shape music communities, music tastes, and the very landscape of the music industry. Therefore, emerging artists who are striving to hit the right notes in their social media journey can learn high notes from these success stories. Keep tuning your social media strategies until they become harmonious symphonies that echo across the digital realm!

Chapter 10. Syncopation with Algorithms: Understanding Analytics to Grow Your Audience

In the harmonious symphony of a musician's social media strategy, understanding algorithms could be likened to knowing the score before an orchestra begins to play. Our journey into this complex landscape begins by understanding, at a broad level, what social media analytics and algorithms are, and how they affect your digital presence and growth.

10.1. The World of Analytics: A Brief Introduction

Social media analytics is an essential tool in your online toolbox as a musician. It is akin to the rhythm section of your band, providing the pulsing backbone. In the context of social media, think of analytics as a set of data points that offer insights into how your content is performing, who your audience is, where they are from, and how they interact with your digital persona. These data points, when interpreted correctly, can be incredibly powerful - they are the concertmasters of the digital stage, dictating reactions, controlling dynamics, and dictating tempo.

In the realm of different social media platforms, each one provides its unique set of analytical tools: Facebook Insights, Instagram Insights, Twitter Analytics, and YouTube Studio, for instance. Just as you would learn your scales on a new instrument, it is pivotal to familiarize yourself with these robust tools to make the most of them.

10.2. Demystifying Algorithms

Algorithms are the conductors of the social media orchestra. Just like a conductor can control the tempo, volume, and the overall direction of an orchestra, algorithms can control the visibility, reach, and the overall performance of your posts based on a myriad of factors.

When a user logs into their social media account, algorithms work behind the scenes to curate a personalized feed, selecting from billions of posts based on the platform's understanding of that user's preferences. 'Preferences' here could be anything - people the user commonly engages with, the type of content they frequently interact with, or even the duration for which they typically browse - the factors are as numerous and diverse as the notes you might play in a virtuosic solo.

The intricacies of these algorithms are carefully guarded secrets, updated frequently, and differ from platform to platform - Facebook's algorithm isn't exactly the same as Instagram's or YouTube's. However, they share common principles that, when understood and applied can help burgeoning musicians like you to fine-tune your posts for maximum visibility and engagement.

10.3. Align Your Post Frequencies with the Beat of Algorithms

One fundamental principle to bear in mind is that algorithms favor regularity - akin to the consistency required to maintain the rhythm in a musical piece. This means that a musician who frequently posts high-quality content is likely to be rewarded with higher visibility, as compared to one who posts sporadically.

However, this doesn't mean you should inundate your followers with posts. It merely underscores the necessity of a regular, consistent schedule. Posting too frequently might result in content fatigue for your followers, dulling their interest in your future posts. The ideal frequency will vary depending on the platform you're focusing on and your target audience's preferences and behavior, an understanding of which can be gleaned from in-depth analytics.

10.4. Create Bidirectional Engagement for an Encore

Just as a riveting performance encourages applause, producing engaging content encourages interaction. Your followers' likes, shares, comments, saves, reposts, all function as a resounding applause in the virtual ecosystem. Why? Because algorithms perceive this engagement as an indicator of user interest and value.

In most cases, the more engagement a post initiates, the more prominently it will feature in your followers' feeds. You can amplify this effect by engaging back with your audience - by responding to comments, liking their responses, and even engaging with their content.

10.5. Play to Your Strengths: Leveraging Engagement Data

Utilizing the insights provided through social media analytics, you can identify which types of posts evoke the most engagement. These metrics, akin to the applause at the end of a concert, can guide you as to what resonates most with your audience. Was it the teaser video of your upcoming album, the behind-the-scenes photos from your studio, or the live Q&A session you hosted? The more you understand what catches your audience's attention, the more effectively you can tailor your content to consistently elicit a standing ovation.

The journey through social media analytics and algorithms is akin to learning a new, intricate musical piece. It can be complex, a little overwhelming, but with patience, practice, and perseverance, you can master it. Understanding analytics and algorithms is an essential step in growing your audience, increasing your reach, and turning the spotlight on your musical journey. With the rhythm of the digital realm in your hands, who knows the dizzy heights your melody can reach?

Chapter 11. The Grand Finale: Developing a Sustainable Long-Term Social Media Strategy

Welcome to the culmination of your social media education thus far. While each stage of your growth has necessitated its own strategies and adaptability paradigms, the essence of this journey has been to equip you with the essential tools required to sculpt your digital destiny. Now we delve deep into the final segment of your expedition.

Your engagements, content creation, platform navigation, and collaborative ventures have all curated a holistic approach to your music's propagation in the digital realm. The Grand Finale aims at synthesizing all these elements into a sustainable, long-term social media strategy that strikes the perfect chord with your vision as an artist.

11.1. Creating a Social Media Calendar

In the realm of social media, consistency is key. Irrespective of the platform, ensuring regular visibility to your audience is crucial to keep them engaged over the long run. A social media calendar comes to your rescue.

The calendar should incorporate a combination of different types of content such as live performances, collaborations, behind-the-scenes, updates about forthcoming projects, and more. Following a calendar not only helps maintain an organized approach towards posting but also provides a structured path to your followers, leaving them in anticipation of what's coming next.

A myriad of online tools and applications out there can assist you in creating and managing your social media calendar, Google Sheets and Hootsuite being popular examples amongst them.

11.2. Long-Term Engagement Strategies

Engaging with your audience is not a one-time event, but rather an ongoing relationship. Building a rapport with your community serves as the backbone to any sustainable social media strategy.

Incorporating daily interactions with fans, regularly responding to comments, encouraging fan-creations and dedications, and orchestrating virtual meet-and-greets or live Q/A sessions can significantly enhance your bond with your audience. A consistent and continued engagement exercise helps build a loyal fan base that sticks around and grows with you over an extended period.

11.3. Aligning with the Algorithm

Algorithms are not as daunting as they may seem initially. They follow specific patterns based on user behavior and engagement metrics. Understanding these patterns can help you optimize your content for greater reach and engagement.

Consistently analyzing your performance based on the metrics provided by each platform is crucial. Such an informed approach can help you adapt and refine your tactics to better align with algorithmic trends, ensuring a sustained visibility and engagement in the digital crowd.

11.4. Leveraging Trends

Viral content can sometimes feel like a lightning strike—powerful but fleeting. However, adopting a strategic approach towards leveraging trends can augment consistent growth. It's crucial to discern between trends that align with your authentic self-expression as a musician versus those that might give you temporary popularity but not long-term, loyal followership.

Dedicating resources towards identifying and capitalizing on current and upcoming trends can significantly enhance your social media longevity.

11.5. Collaborations: The Long Game

Collaborations aren't a flash-in-the-pan moment of shared glory between artists. They are, in fact, a powerful networking tool that can create a ripple effect, reaching far wider audiences than you could achieve on your own.

The long-term strategy here should involve identifying potential collaborators who align with your branding and musical ethos, having regular co-projects, and even forming long-lasting partnerships.

11.6. Adapting and Evolving: The Social Media Dances

The ever-evolving landscape of social media ensures that staying agile and adapting quickly is paramount to any sustainable strategy. Your practices should be under constant review and open to refinements.

Monitoring changing audience preferences, new platform features, and shifting cultural nuances are all part of the dance. Crafting a strategy that is flexible enough to weather these changes is the ultimate finale to your social media mastery.

In conclusion, developing a sustainable long-term social media strategy requires a synthesis of numerous elements: consistent engagement, strategic content planning, fine-tuned understanding of platform algorithms, astute trend utilization, effective collaborations, and a nimble approach towards the ever-changing panorama of social media. Each aspect requires equal attention and diligent nurturing to resonate with your vision as a musician and accelerate your journey towards social media eminence. Embrace this journey, strike your unique chord and witness the powerful symphony you can create in the expansive digital concert hall of social media.